PRAYERS
New and Old

revised edition

Forward Movement Publications
Cincinnati, Ohio, USA

This revised edition of

Prayers New and Old

is

lovingly and gratefully dedicated to

CHARLES HENRY LONG

Priest ✝ Missionary

Director and Editor of

FORWARD MOVEMENT PUBLICATIONS

1978-1994

✝

While we have breath, therefore,
let us rejoice in one another,
For a small part in God's great master plan,
For the mystery of His love for us,
Our hopeful prayer for one more year
Of health and grace and peace.

— CHL
Advent 1999

Prayers New and Old has been in print, with minor changes, since 1937 and has sold more than 1,750,000 copies.

Forward Movement Publications

412 Sycamore Street, Cincinnati, Ohio 45202
©2000

Contents

THE LORD'S PRAYER

Our Father, who art in heaven, hallowed be thy Name, thy kingdom come, thy will be done, on earth as it is in heaven. Give us this day our daily bread. And forgive us our trespasses, as we forgive those who trespass against us. And lead us not into temptation, but deliver us from evil. For thine is the kingdom, and the power, and the glory, for ever and ever. Amen.

THE APOSTLES' CREED

I believe in God the Father Almighty, Maker of heaven and earth:

And in Jesus Christ his only Son our Lord: Who was conceived by the Holy Ghost, Born of the Virgin Mary, Suffered under Pontius Pilate, Was crucified, dead and buried. He descended into hell; The third day he rose again from the dead: He ascended into heaven, And sitteth on the right hand of God the Father Almighty: From thence he shall come to judge the quick and the dead.

I believe in the Holy Ghost: The holy Catholic Church, The Communion of Saints, The Forgiveness of sins: The Resurrection of the body: And the Life everlasting. Amen.

THE COMMANDMENTS

God spake these words, and said:

I am the Lord thy God who brought thee out of the land of Egypt, out of the house of bondage. Thou shalt have none other gods but me.

Lord, have mercy upon us, and incline our hearts to keep this law.

Thou shalt not make to thyself any graven image, nor the likeness of any thing that is in heaven above, or in the earth beneath, or in the water under the earth; thou shalt not bow down to them, nor worship them.

Lord, have mercy upon us...

Thou shalt not take the Name of the Lord thy God in vain.

Lord, have mercy upon us...

Remember that thou keep holy the Sabbath day.

Lord, have mercy upon us...

Honor thy father and thy mother.

Lord, have mercy upon us...

Thou shalt do no murder.

Lord, have mercy upon us...

Thou shalt not commit adultery.

Lord, have mercy upon us...

Thou shalt not steal.

Lord, have mercy upon us...

Thou shalt not bear false witness against thy neighbor.

Lord, have mercy upon us...

Thou shalt not covet.

Lord, have mercy upon us, and write all these thy laws in our hearts, we beseech thee.

Hear what our Lord Jesus Christ saith:

Thou shalt love the Lord thy God with all thy heart, and with all thy soul, and with all thy mind. This is the first and great commandment. And the second is like unto it: thou shalt love thy neighbor as thyself. On these two commandments hang all the Law and the Prophets.

Family Prayers

FOR A HAPPY HOME

O loving Father, bless our home. Fill it with the gladness of your presence, that we may all be happy in your love and in our love for each other. May Jesus, your Son, be our loved and honored Guest, sharing our joys and comforting our sorrows.

O God, whose desire is that all the peoples of the world should be one human family, living together in harmony, grant that our home, by its worship and its witness, may help to hasten the day when your will is done on earth as it is in heaven.

A MARRIED COUPLE'S PRAYER

Eternal God, so knit our wills together with your will that we may grow in love and peace with you and with each other. Give us grace, when we hurt each other, to seek each other's forgiveness and yours. Make our life together a sign of Christ's love to this sinful and broken world, and grant that we may reach out in love and concern for others; through Jesus Christ our Lord.

PARENTS' THANKSGIVING

We thank you, God our Father, for giving us our *child(ren)* to bring up for you. Help us as true disciples to set *them* a good example in all we think or say or do. Keep *them* healthy in body and mind; and grant that *they* may grow in grace and in the knowledge and love of your Son, our Savior, Jesus Christ.

FOR A BIRTHDAY

O God, grant that the year ahead for _____ may be one of newness, hope, joy and unexpected surprises. May your truth light *his* path, and may *his* life grow more fully into yours; through Jesus Christ our Lord.

ON THE ANNIVERSARY OF A BAPTISM

Grant, O Lord, that as we have been received into the household of God, signed with the sign of the Cross, and marked as Christ's own for ever, we may never fear to confess the faith of Christ crucified, proclaim his resurrection, and share in his eternal priesthood.

ON THE ANNIVERSARY
OF A CONFIRMATION

O Lord, defend us with your heavenly grace, and increase in us your Holy Spirit more and more, that we may continue yours for ever. Strengthen us and send us forth in the power of the Spirit to persevere in your service until we come to your everlasting kingdom.

ON THE ANNIVERSARY
OF ONE DEPARTED

Father of all, we remember before you today your servant, ___, whom we love but see no longer. Grant *him* your peace and let light perpetual shine upon *him*. Grant that we, too, may at length fall asleep peacefully in you and wake up in the likeness of your Son, Jesus Christ our Lord.

FOR THOSE WE LOVE

Almighty God, we entrust all who are dear to us to your never-failing care and love, for this life and the life to come, knowing that you are doing for them better things than we can either desire or pray for; through Jesus Christ our Lord.

FOR ABSENT LOVED ONES

O God, whose fatherly care *reacheth* to the uttermost parts of the earth: We humbly beseech *thee* graciously to behold and bless those whom we love, now absent from us. Defend them from all dangers of soul and body; and grant that both they and we, drawing nearer to *thee,* may be bound together by *thy* love in the communion of *thy* Holy Spirit, and in the fellowship of *thy* saints; through Jesus Christ our Lord.

PRAYERS TO USE WITH
SMALL CHILDREN

[Before children can talk, parents may pray in their presence, and they will come to accept prayer as a normal part of life. When they are old enough to speak, they may be encouraged to join in short rhymed or rhythmic prayers, and to pray in their own words, using simple outlines such as:

Thank you God, for . . . .

Lord Jesus Christ, be with me today . . . .

Dear God, bless . . . .]

IN THE MORNING

Lord Jesus bless me when I rise,
Bless the day that meets my eyes.
Bless the daily tasks I do,
With happiness to share with you.

DURING THE DAY

Help me to work
Help me to play.
Help me to learn a bit each day.

I am the child of God.
I ought to do His will.
I can do what He tells me to
And by his grace I will.

AT BEDTIME

Lord Jesus, watch me when I sleep,
For my life is yours to keep.
Waking, sleeping, with a prayer,
Safely in your loving care.

Lord, keep us safe this night,
Secure from all our fears;
May angels guard us while we sleep
Till morning light appears.

A CHILD'S FAITH

I believe in God above,
I believe in Jesus' love,
I believe his Spirit, too,
Comes to teach me what to do.
I believe that I can be
True and loving, Lord, like thee.

A CHILD'S PRAISE

Praise be to God
The dear Father who made me.

Praise to the Son
The Lord Jesus who saved me.

Praise to the Spirit
For power which he gives me.

Most Holy Trinity
Help and defend me.

FOR PRAYER

Teach me to pray dear Lord, teach me to pray,
Not only to say my prayers, but really to pray.
Others dear Lord can tell me what to say,
But only you can lead me on to pray.

For Daily Devotions

IN THE MORNING

From Psalm 51

Open my lips, O Lord,*
    and my mouth shall proclaim your praise.
Create in me a clean heart, O God,*
    and renew a right spirit within me.
Cast me not away from your presence*
    and take not your holy Spirit from me.
Give me the joy of your saving help again*
    and sustain me with your bountiful Spirit.
Glory to the Father, and to the Son and to
        the Holy Spirit:*
    as it was in the beginning, is now,
    and will be for ever. Amen.

A Reading

Blessed be the God and Father of our Lord
Jesus Christ! By his great mercy we have
been born anew to a living hope through the
resurrection of Jesus Christ from the dead.

— *1 Peter 1:3*

Prayers may be offered for ourselves and others.

The Lord's Prayer

The Collect

Lord God, almighty and everlasting Father, you have brought us in safety to this new day: Preserve us with your mighty power, that we may not fall into sin, nor be overcome by adversity; and in all we do, direct us to the fulfilling of your purpose; through Jesus Christ our Lord. Amen.

AT NOON

From Psalm 113

Give praise, you servants of the Lord;*
    praise the Name of the Lord.
Let the Name of the Lord be blessed,*
    from this time forth for evermore.
From the rising of the sun to its going down*
    let the Name of the Lord be praised.
The Lord is high above all nations,*
    and his glory above the heavens.

A Reading

O God, you will keep in perfect peace those whose minds are fixed on you; for in returning and rest we shall be saved; in quietness and trust shall be our strength.   — *Isaiah 26:3; 30:15*

Prayers may be offered for ourselves and others.

The Lord's Prayer

The Collect

Blessed Savior, at this hour you hung upon
the cross, stretching out your loving arms:
Grant that all the peoples of the earth may
look to you and be saved; for your mercies'
sake.

or this

Lord Jesus Christ, you said to your apostles,
"Peace I give to you; my own peace I leave
with you:" Regard not our sins, but the faith
of your Church, and give to us the peace and
unity of that heavenly City, where with the
Father and the Holy Spirit you live and reign,
now and for ever. *Amen.*

IN THE EARLY EVENING

O gracious Light,
pure brightness of the everliving Father in
    heaven,
O Jesus Christ, holy and blessed!

Now as we come to the setting of the sun,
and our eyes behold the vesper light,

we sing your praises O God: Father, Son,
and Holy Spirit.

You are worthy at all times to be praised
by happy voices,
O Son of God, O Giver of life,
and to be glorified through all the world.

A Reading

It is not ourselves that we proclaim; we
proclaim Christ Jesus as Lord, and ourselves
as your servants, for Jesus' sake. For the
same God who said, "Out of darkness let
light shine," has caused his light to shine
within us, to give the light of revelation — the
revelation of the glory of God in the face of
Jesus Christ.   *— 2 Corinthians 4:5-6*

Prayers may be offered for ourselves and others.

The Lord's Prayer

The Collect

Lord Jesus, stay with us, for evening is at
hand and the day is past; be our companion in
the way, kindle our hearts, and awaken hope,
that we may know you as you are revealed in
Scripture and in the breaking of bread. Grant
this for the sake of your love.

AT THE CLOSE OF DAY

Psalm 134

Behold now, bless the Lord, all you
       servants of the Lord,*
  you that stand by night in the house of
  the Lord.

Lift up your hands in the holy place and
       bless the Lord;*
  the Lord who made heaven and earth
  bless you out of Zion.

A Reading

Lord, you are in the midst of us and we are
called by your Name: Do not forsake us, O
Lord our God.   *— Jeremiah 14:9, 22*

The following may be said

The Song of Simeon *Nunc dimittis*
Luke 2:29-32

Lord, now lettest thou thy servant depart in
       peace,*
  according to thy word;

For mine eyes have seen thy salvation,*
  which thou hast prepared before the face
  of all people,

To be a light to lighten the Gentiles,*
    and to be the glory of thy people Israel.

Prayers for ourselves and others may follow. Prayers of thanksgiving for the blessings of the day, and prayers of penitence for our sins may be included.

The Lord's Prayer

The Collect

Visit this place, O Lord, and drive far from it all snares of the enemy; let your holy angels dwell with us to preserve us in peace; and let your blessing be upon us always; through Jesus Christ our Lord. *Amen.*

The almighty and merciful Lord, Father, Son, and Holy Spirit, bless us and keep us. *Amen.*

[*In all forms of Daily Devotions, Scripture readings from the Book of Common Prayer Daily Office Lectionary, from* Forward Day by Day, *or from some other plan of reading may be used. The Collect for the week and other prayers from the prayer book may be added, as well as suitable prayers from this collection.*]

Praise and Thanksgiving

CANTICLE OF THE SUN

Highest, all-powerful, good Lord,
Yours is the praise, the glory, and the honor,
And every blessing.
They belong to you alone, Most High,
And no one is worthy to speak your name.

So, praised be you, my Lord, with all
    your creatures,
Especially Brother Sun,
Who makes the day and enlightens us
    through you.
He is lovely and radiant and grand;
And he heralds you, his Most High Lord.

Praised be you, my Lord, through Sister
    Moon
And the stars.
You have hung them in heaven shining and
    precious and fair.

Praise to you, my Lord,
Through those who forgive one another in
    your love,
Who bear sickness and trials.

Blessed are they who live in peace,
For they will be crowned by you, Most High!

O praise and bless my Lord,
Thank him and serve him.

A SONG TO THE LAMB

Splendor and honor and kingly power are
   yours by right, O Lord our God,
For you created everything that is, and by
   your will they were created and have
   their being.
And yours by right, O Lamb that was slain,
   for with your blood you have redeemed
   for God,
From every family, language, people,
   and nation, a kingdom of priests to serve
   our God.
And so, to him who sits upon the throne,
   and to Christ the Lamb,
Be worship and praise, dominion and
   splendor, for ever and for evermore.

SONG OF ZECHARIAH

Blessed be the Lord, the God of Israel;
  he has come to his people and set them
  free.
He has raised up for us a mighty savior,
  born of the house of his servant David.
Through his holy prophets he promised of
  old,
that he would save us from our enemies,
  from the hands of all who hate us.
He promised to show mercy to our fathers
  and to remember his holy covenant.

— Luke 1:68-72

FOR LITTLE BLESSINGS

O heavenly Father, we thank you for all the
blessings that we take for granted: for life as
we awake each morning, for a task to be done
this day, for rain that we may drink, for food
that we may eat, for a home to return to at
day's end so that we may rest, and for so
many more little blessings that are not shared
by millions in our world, and to whom our
little blessings would loom large. Dear God,
make us thankful in all ways, always.

— Beulah H. Gardner

THE GENERAL THANKSGIVING

Almighty God, Father of all mercies, we thine unworthy servants do give thee most humble and hearty thanks for all thy goodness and loving-kindness to us and to all men. We bless thee for our creation, preservation, and all the blessings of this life; but above all for thine inestimable love in the redemption of the world by our Lord Jesus Christ; for the means of grace, and for the hope of glory. And, we beseech thee, give us that due sense of all thy mercies, that our hearts may be unfeignedly thankful; and that we show forth thy praise, not only with our lips, but in our lives, by giving up our selves to thy service, and by walking before thee in holiness and righteousness all our days; through Jesus Christ our Lord, to whom, with thee and the Holy Ghost, be all honor and glory, world without end. Amen.

FOR THE GIFT OF LIFE

Bountiful God, accept our thankfulness for the creation and gift of life, ours and the animals and plants. May highest praise ever rise from your fertile blue and green planet, spinning in the beauty of your order, by your eternal grace.

FOR GOD'S BEST GIFTS

O God of Love, we praise you for all your servants who by their example and encouragement have helped us on our way, and for every vision of you which you have ever given us in sacrament or prayer; and we pray that we may use these gifts in your service and to the glory of your Holy Name.

GRACES FOR CHILDREN

God is great, God is good,
And we thank him for our food.

God bless our meat,
God guide our ways,
God give us grace
Our Lord to please.   — *George Bellin, 1565*

GRACE AT MEALS

Bless, O Lord, this food to our use, and us to thy service, and make us ever mindful of the needs of others.

Blessed are you, Lord our God, ruler of the universe; we have shared of your bounty, and through your goodness we live.

Come, Lord Jesus, be our guest, and let these gifts to us be blessed.

A TWELFTH CENTURY PRAYER

Thanks be to thee, my Lord Jesus Christ,
For all the benefits thou hast given me,
For all the pains and insults thou hast borne
   for me.
O most merciful Redeemer, Friend and
   Brother,
May I know thee more clearly,
Love thee more dearly, and
Follow thee more nearly,
Day by day.

— *St. Richard of Chichester*

WE PRAISE THEE

We praise thee, O God; we acknowledge
            thee to be the Lord.
All the earth doth worship thee, the Father
            everlasting.
To thee all Angels cry aloud,
the Heavens and all the Powers therein.
To thee Cherubim and Seraphim
            continually do cry:

Holy, holy, holy, Lord God of Sabaoth;
Heaven and earth are full of the majesty
of thy glory.
The glorious company of the apostles
praise thee.
The goodly fellowship of the prophets
praise thee.
The noble army of martyrs praise thee.
The holy Church throughout all the world
doth acknowledge thee,
the Father, of an infinite majesty,
thine adorable, true, and only Son,
also the Holy Ghost the Comforter.

Thou art the King of glory, O Christ.
Thou art the everlasting Son of the Father.
When thou tookest upon thee to deliver man,
thou didst humble thyself to be born of a
Virgin.
When thou hadst overcome the sharpness
of death,
thou didst open the kingdom of heaven to
all believers.
Thou sittest at the right hand of God, in the
glory of the Father.
We believe that thou shalt come to be our
judge.
We therefore pray thee, help thy servants,

whom thou hast redeemed with thy
>precious blood.
Make them to be numbered with thy saints,
in glory everlasting.

— *Te Deum laudamus*

A LITANY OF THANKSGIVING

Let us give thanks to God our Father for all
his gifts so freely bestowed upon us.

For the beauty and wonder of your
creation, in earth and sky and sea,

We thank you Lord.

For all that is gracious in the lives of men
and women, revealing the image of Christ,

We thank you Lord.

For our daily food and drink, our homes
and families, and our friends,

We thank you Lord.

For minds to think, and hearts to love, and
hands to serve,

We thank you Lord.

For health and strength to work, and leisure
to rest and play,

We thank you Lord.

For the brave and courageous, who are patient in suffering and faithful in adversity,

We thank you Lord.

For all valiant seekers after truth, liberty, and justice,

We thank you Lord.

For the communion of saints, in all times and places,

We thank you Lord.

Above all, we give you thanks for the great mercies and promises given to us in Christ Jesus our Lord;

To him be praise and glory, with you, O Father, and the Holy Spirit, now and forever.

Amen.

For Individual Needs

A MORNING PRAYER

O God, I give this day to thee.
Bless it and give it back to me
That I may use it all for thee,
For Jesus' sake—so may it be.

FOR GOD'S PRESENCE
THROUGH THE DAY

Teach me, O God, how to take the gift of a day and give it back to you, radiant in faith, spontaneous in joy, and rich in service.

O Lord, be with me today and grant me the wisdom of a loving heart in everything I say and do. Help me to listen to everyone who talks with me and to care for their feelings. Make me ready both to do and to receive little acts of kindness.

Grant, O Lord, that whether this day is outwardly joyous or sad, as I go about my daily work I may fix my thoughts and efforts on whatever is true, whatever is honest, whatever is just, whatever is lovely, and whatever is of good report.

Lord, you are in the midst of us, and we are called by your Name: Do not forsake us, O Lord our God.

O Lord, support us all the day long, until the shadows lengthen, and the evening comes, and the busy world is hushed, and the fever of life is over, and our work is done. Then in your mercy, grant us a safe lodging and a holy rest, and peace at the last.

I lie down in peace; at once I fall asleep; for only you, Lord, make me dwell in safety.

Guide us waking, O Lord, and guard us sleeping; that awake we may watch with Christ, and asleep we may rest in peace.

Savior of the world, by your cross and precious blood you have redeemed us; Save us, and help us, we humbly beseech you, O Lord.

FOR REFRESHMENT
IN DAILY LIFE

O God, in sunshine and rain, in work and rest, in friendship and solitude, in the common things of life you give us your very self, making bread and wine the Sacrament of your sustaining presence: strengthen and refresh us, that we may eagerly seek you, surely find you, and faithfully serve you, through Jesus Christ our Lord.

FOR GOD'S MERCY

Almighty and everlasting God, you are always more ready to hear than we to pray, and to give more than we either desire or deserve: Pour upon us the abundance of your mercy, forgiving us those things of which our conscience is afraid, and giving us those good things for which we are not worthy to ask, except through the merits and mediation of Jesus Christ our Savior; who lives and reigns with you and the Holy Spirit, one God, for ever and ever.

Soul of Christ, sanctify me;
Body of Christ, save me;
Blood of Christ, refresh me;
Water from the side of Christ, wash me;
Passion of Christ, strengthen me;
O good Jesus, hear me;
Within thy wounds hide me;
Suffer me not to be separated from thee;
From the malicious enemy defend me;
In the hour of my death call me,
And bid me come to thee,
That with thy Saints I may praise thee
For ever and ever.

O God, the protector of all who trust in you, without whom nothing is strong, nothing is holy: Increase and multiply upon us your mercy; that, with you as our ruler and guide, we may so pass through things temporal, that we lose not the things eternal; through Jesus Christ our Lord, who lives and reigns with you and the Holy Spirit, one God, for ever and ever.

FOR THE SPIRIT
OF FORGIVENESS

Jesus, strong and gentle, keep me patient
for love of thee.

Jesus, generous and forgiving, help me to
forgive as thou hast forgiven me.

Gracious God, we know your power to
triumph over weakness. May we who ask
forgiveness be ready to forgive one another,
in the name of Jesus the Lord.

A CONFESSION

Almighty God, our heavenly Father: we have
sinned against you, through our own fault, in
thought, and word, and deed, and in what we
have left undone. For the sake of your Son
our Lord Jesus Christ, forgive us all our
offenses; and grant that we may serve you in
newness of life, to the glory of your Name.

ABSOLUTION

May almighty God grant us forgiveness of all
our sins and the grace and comfort of the
Holy Spirit.

FOR THE SPIRIT OF PRAYER

Lord, amid the noise and stress of daily life, help us to preserve a silence within. In moments of crisis may we turn to you, the center of our being, to find you awaiting us. Bless us with the vision of your change-lessness and grant us peace; through Jesus Christ our Lord.

FOR PURITY OF HEART

Almighty God, to you all hearts are open, all desires known, and from you no secrets are hid: Cleanse the thoughts of our hearts by the inspiration of your Holy Spirit, that we may perfectly love you, and worthily magnify your holy Name; through Jesus Christ our Lord.

FOR A PURE INTENTION

O God, give us a pure heart, a clear mind, and a steadfast will, that all our work may be to the honor of him who has honored us with his love and fellowship, Jesus Christ our Lord.

FOR SANCTIFICATION

Remember, O Lord, what you have wrought in us and not what we deserve; and, as you have called us to your service, make us worthy of our calling; through Jesus Christ our Lord, who lives and reigns with you and the Holy Spirit, one God now and for ever.

A PRAYER OF
ST. FRANCIS OF ASSISI

Lord, make us instruments of your peace. Where there is hatred, let us sow love; where there is injury, pardon; where there is discord, union; where there is doubt, faith; where there is despair, hope; where there is darkness, light; where there is sadness, joy. Grant that we may not so much seek to be consoled as to console; to be understood as to understand; to be loved as to love. For it is in giving that we receive; it is in pardoning that we are pardoned; and it is in dying that we are born to eternal life.

FOR GUIDANCE

O Compassionate Jesus, friend of sinners, God incarnate, giver of life: thank you for the gift of life. Help me to know what to do and say, so that I may be of service to others in Your Name.

FOR LOVE TOWARD GOD

O God, you have prepared for those who love you such good things as surpass our understanding: Pour into our hearts such love towards you, that we, loving you in all things and above all things, may obtain your promises, which exceed all that we can desire; through Jesus Christ our Lord, who lives and reigns with you and the Holy Spirit, one God for ever and ever.

FOR SELF-DEDICATION

Gracious God, help us by your Holy Spirit to walk in your will and to love with Christ's love, that our lives may find a simple harmony with your purposes and, quieted by prayer, lighten the world's need, ever singing your praise.

FOR FIDELITY

Teach us, good Lord, to serve you as you deserve; to give and not to count the cost; to fight and not to heed the wounds; to toil and not to seek for rest; to labor and not to ask for any reward save that of knowing that we are doing your will; through Jesus Christ our Lord.

FOR DISCIPLESHIP

Heavenly Father, may we learn more and more to live each day under your direction and guidance, according to your will, knowing that you will not fail to provide vision, understanding, strength, wisdom, and courage to those who are open to receive them; for the sake of your dear Son, Jesus Christ.

FOR GOD'S PROTECTION

Almighty and merciful God, in your goodness keep us, we pray, from all things that may hurt us, that we, being ready both in mind and body, may accomplish with free hearts those things which belong to your purpose; through Jesus Christ our Lord, who lives and reigns with you and the Holy Spirit, one God, now and for ever.

FOR DELIVERANCE FROM EVIL

Lord God, in the beginning of creation you called forth light to dispel the darkness that lay upon the face of the deep: Deliver your servants from the powers of evil and illumine us with the light of your presence, that with open eyes and glad hearts we may worship you and serve you, now and for ever; through Jesus Christ our Lord.

FOR DIVINE DIRECTION

Direct us, O Lord, in all our doings with your most gracious favor, and further us with your continual help; that in all our works begun, continued, and ended in you, we may glorify your holy Name, and finally, by your mercy, obtain everlasting life; through Jesus Christ our Lord.

Lord Christ, true Light who enlightens every one: Shine in our hearts that we may clearly see the way that leads to life eternal, and may follow without stumbling; for you are the Way, O Christ, as you are the Truth and the Life; and you live and reign for ever and ever.

FOR TRUE RELIGION

Lord of all power and might, the author and giver of all good things: Graft in our hearts the love of your Name; increase in us true religion; nourish us with all goodness; and bring forth in us the fruit of good works; through Jesus Christ our Lord, who lives and reigns with you and the Holy Spirit, one God for ever and ever.

AN APPROACH TO CHRIST

To know of thee, O Christ, is eternal life; to see thee is the end of all desire; to serve thee is perfect freedom and everlasting joy.

FOR THE PRESENCE OF CHRIST

Lord, you manifested yourself to your disciples at Emmaus in the breaking of bread: grant us through the same Blessed Sacrament of your presence to know and to love you with all our hearts. Abide with us, that we may ever abide in you.

O living Christ, touch our eyes that we may see you; open our ears that we may hear you; enter our hearts that we may know you.

FOR THE SPIRIT
OF SERVICE

Almighty God, your Son Jesus Christ has taught us that what we do for the least of your children we do also for him: Give us the will to serve others as he was servant of all, who lives and reigns with you and the Holy Spirit, one God, now and for ever.

FOR REST IN THE LORD

Keep us, Lord, awake in the duties of our callings, yet grant that we may sleep in thy peace.

FOR GUIDANCE
OF THE HOLY SPIRIT

O God, because without you we are not able to please you, mercifully grant that your Holy Spirit may in all things direct and rule our hearts; through Jesus Christ our Lord, who lives and reigns with you and the Holy Spirit, one God, now and for ever.

FOR CONSECRATION

O God, light of the minds that seek thee, life of the souls that love thee, and strength of the hearts that hope in thee: enlarge our minds and raise the vision of our hearts that our spirits may reach thee, the eternal Wisdom, with swift wings of thought, who art from everlasting to everlasting.

THE SERENITY PRAYER

God, grant me the Serenity to accept the things I cannot change, Courage to change the things I can, and Wisdom to know the difference.

— Reinhold Neibuhr

IN SICKNESS

O God, the source of all health: So fill my heart with faith in your love, that with calm expectancy I may make room for your presence, and gracefully accept your healing; through Jesus Christ our Lord.

Lord, sanctify my sickness. May my weakness add strength to my faith and seriousness to my repentance. Grant that I may live with you in everlasting life; through Jesus Christ our Lord.

ST. TERESA'S PRAYER

Nada te turbe;
Nada te espante;
Todo se pasa;
Dios no se muda;
La paciencia todo lo alcanza.
Quien a Dios tiene, nada le falta.
Solo Dios basta.

Let nothing trouble thee;
Let nothing afright thee;
All things are passing,
    God never changes;
    Patience obtains everything,
Nothing is wanting to him
    who possesses God.
God alone suffices.

FOR STEADFASTNESS

O Almighty God, who alone canst order the unruly wills and affections of sinners, grant unto thy people that they may love the thing which thou commandest, and desire that which thou dost promise; that so, among the sundry and manifold changes of the world, our hearts may surely there be fixed, where true joys are to be found; through Jesus Christ our Lord.

FOR COURAGE TO PERSEVERE

O God, you have called us to your service; show us your purpose for our lives; though it be hard, make us long to follow it; and give us courage to persevere until, at the last, we reach the goal which you have set for us; through Jesus Christ our Lord.

FOR COURAGE AND STRENGTH

If I tend to fold under stress, O God, stir in me the image of Jesus, who stumbled and fell under the weight of his cross, but who rose to carry it to his appointment with you.

Give us courage, O Lord, to stand up and be counted, to stand for those who cannot stand for themselves, and to stand for ourselves when it is needful for us to do so.

FOR SELF-MASTERY

O Lord, help us to be masters of ourselves that we may be the servants of others.

THINKING ABOUT DEATH

Father in heaven, you gave your Son Jesus Christ to suffering and death on the cross, and raised him to life in glory. Grant us a patient faith in time of darkness, and strengthen our hearts with the knowledge of your love; through Jesus Christ our Lord.

Bring us, O Lord God, at our last awakening into the house and gate of heaven, where there shall be no darkness but light; no noise nor silence but music; no end or beginning, but eternity; in the habitations of thy glory and dominion, for ever and ever.

FOR FREEDOM FROM ANXIETY

Most loving Father, whose will it is for us to give thanks for all things, to fear nothing but the loss of you, and to cast all our care on you who care for us: Preserve us from faithless fears and worldly anxieties, that no clouds of this mortal life may hide from us the light of that love which is immortal, and which you have manifested to us in your Son Jesus Christ our Lord; who lives and reigns with you in the unity of the Holy Spirit, one God now and for ever.

FOR AWARENESS
OF GOD'S PURPOSE

Lord God almighty, we are yours and we would serve you. By the power of your Spirit, open our eyes to see the world as you see it; enkindle our hearts that we may share your love for it; enlighten our minds that we may understand your will for it; and grant us grace and strength so to live in it that we may help to make it wholly yours; for the sake of him who lived in it and died for it, and lives forever with you and the Holy Spirit.

FOR WISDOM

O Lord, grant me heavenly wisdom, that I may learn above all things to seek and to find you, to relish and to love you, and to think of all other things as being, as indeed they are, at the disposal of your wisdom.

Grant us, O God, in all our doubts and uncertainties, the grace to ask what you would have us do, that the Spirit of wisdom may save us from all false choices, and that in your light we may see light, and in your straight path may not stumble; through Jesus Christ our Lord.

IN OUR DAILY WORK

The things, good Lord, that we pray for, give us the grace to labor for.

God give me work till my life shall end and life till my work is done.

Lord, temper with tranquility
Our manifold activity,
That we may do our work for thee
In very great simplicity.

Lord God, our heavenly Father, grant that we may sincerely, faithfully and honestly serve you in our daily work. Help us to be obedient, faithful children, like your Son, our brother, Jesus Christ.

FOR CONFIDENT HOPE

Eternal and unchangeable God, in whom alone we find rest for our weariness and comfort for our sorrow, and from whom alone cometh all true joy; keep our hearts, we beseech thee, ever fixed on thee through life and death, waiting patiently for that glorious day when we shall rejoice in the fulness of thy love for evermore; through Jesus Christ our Lord.

FOR HUMILITY

Take from us, O Lord God, all pride and vanity, all boasting and self-assertion, and give us true courage that shows itself in gentleness; true wisdom that shows itself in simplicity; and true power that shows itself in modesty; through Jesus Christ our Lord.

FOR CHRISTIAN LOVE

Almighty God, make us gentle and courteous in word and deed. Give us grace to love one another as you have commanded us, and bless our friendships with your Holy Spirit; for the sake of him who loved us and gave himself for us, Jesus Christ our Lord.

FOR HOPE AND COURAGE

O God of hope, fill us, we pray, with all joy and peace in believing, that we may ever abound in hope by the power of your Holy Spirit, and show forth our thankfulness to you in trustful and courageous lives; through Jesus Christ our Lord and Savior.

FOR JOY

O heavenly Father, you have filled the world with beauty: Open our eyes to behold your gracious hand in all your works; that, rejoicing in your whole creation, we may learn to serve you with gladness; for the sake of him through whom all things were made, your Son Jesus Christ our Lord.

FOR THE KNOWLEDGE
AND LOVE OF GOD

O God, our great Companion, you are the light of minds that know you, the life of souls that love you, and the strength of wills that serve you: Help us so to know you that we may truly love you, so to love you that we may fully serve you, and in serving you, know perfect freedom; through Jesus Christ our Lord.

FOR KINDNESS

Grant, O Lord, that in all the joy of life I may never forget to be kind. Help me to be unselfish in friendship, thoughtful of those less fortunate than myself, and eager to share the burdens of others; through Jesus Christ our Savior.

FOR GOD'S GRACE

Lord, we pray that your grace may always precede and follow us, that we may continually be given to good works, through Jesus Christ our Lord, who lives and reigns with you and the Holy Spirit, one God now and for ever.

A PROPHET'S PRAYER

Lord, you have shown us what is good; enable us now, we pray, to do justice, to love kindness, and to walk humbly with you.

GOD IN EVERYDAY LIFE

O God, open our eyes to wider horizons than we have imagined, and unstop our ears to hear your voice in unexpected places. Enlighten our hearts to know your presence, that we may be freed from our self-centeredness and find you everywhere and in all your children; through Jesus Christ our Lord.

A COMMENDATION

Let thy fatherly hand ever be over us; let thy Holy Spirit ever be with us; and so lead us in the knowledge and obedience of thy Word that in the end we may obtain everlasting life; through Jesus Christ our Lord.

FOR HELP IN THE
SEARCH FOR TRUTH

From the cowardice that dares not face
    new truth,
From the laziness that is content with
    half truth,
From the arrogance that thinks it knows
    all truth,
Good Lord, deliver me.

Grant, O Lord, that when our minds are perplexed and we cannot find you, our search for truth will lead us to you.

FOR CONTROL OF SPEECH

O God, you know how often we sin against you by failing to tame our tongues: Keep us from untrue and unkind words; consecrate our speech to your service, and keep us often silent, so that we may listen for your voice; through Jesus Christ our Lord.

FOR STUDENTS OF GOD'S WORD

O gracious and most merciful Father, who hast vouchsafed us the rich and precious jewel of thy holy word: Assist us with thy Spirit that it may be written in our hearts to our everlasting comfort, to reform us, to renew us according to thine own image, to build us up into the perfect building of thy Christ, and to increase in us all heavenly virtues.

Almighty God, your word is a lantern to our feet and a light upon our path; grant that in prayerful reading of the Holy Scriptures we may realize our fellowship with you and with one another; through Jesus Christ your incarnate Word.

FOR UNDERSTANDING
OF THE SCRIPTURES

Blessed Lord, who caused all Holy Scriptures to be written for our learning: Grant us so to hear them, read, mark, learn and inwardly digest them, that we may embrace and ever hold fast the blessed hope of everlasting life, which you have given us in our Savior Jesus Christ; who lives and reigns with you and the Holy Spirit, one God, for ever and ever.

AT EARLY EUCHARIST

As watchmen look for the morning, so do we look for thee, O Christ. Come with the dawning day, and make thyself known to us in the breaking of bread, for thou art our God for ever and ever.

BEFORE HOLY COMMUNION

Incline our hearts, O God, that by the grace of thy Holy Spirit we may worthily approach these sacred mysteries and offer ourselves to thee in answering love, through Jesus Christ our Lord.

AFTER HOLY COMMUNION

God our Father, whose Son our Lord Jesus Christ in a wonderful sacrament has left us a memorial of his passion: Grant us so to venerate the sacred mysteries of his Body and Blood, that we may ever perceive within ourselves the fruit of his redemption; who lives and reigns with you and the Holy Spirit, one God, for ever and ever.

FOR GOOD STEWARDSHIP

O Lord, who hast taught us that thou wilt require much from those to whom much is given, grant that we whom thou hast called to so goodly a heritage may share more abundantly with others what we so richly enjoy, and in serving them may know the glory of serving thee.

IN GOD'S PRESENCE

Sanctify, O Lord, both our coming in and our going forth. Grant that when we leave your house we may not leave your presence, but be ever near to us and keep us near to you, through Jesus Christ our Lord.

FOR OURSELVES
AS WE GROW OLDER

O God, our Father, help us to make use of our later years with cheerfulness and joy, not lamenting our loss of strength, nor afraid of what the years may bring. Give us thankful hearts for all that makes old age less anxious and more secure. If we must suffer at the end, help us to receive gladly all that is done for us.

THE SEVEN VIRTUES

Faith

Hope

Love

Justice

Prudence

Temperance

Fortitude

Intercessions

FOR A WITNESSING CHURCH

Almighty God, you call your church to witness that in Christ we are reconciled to you. Help us so to proclaim the good news of your love, that all who hear it may turn to you.

Lord, pour out your Spirit on the church, that we may show to the people of this land the glory and the power and the truth of the everlasting gospel. Teach us to witness to your love in a greedy society, to witness to your peace in a troubled society, that the men and women of this generation may praise you for your mighty work and live by grace, for Jesus Christ's sake.

FOR THE UNIVERSAL CHURCH

O God, in whose image we are made, and in whose earthly family there is neither Jew nor Greek, male nor female, bond nor free; may your church be enlivened by your love and show to the world the unity to which you have called it in the gospel of your Son, Jesus Christ our Lord.

FOR GOOD S[...]

O Lord Jesus Christ, the [...]
who laid down your life for th[...]
sustain them with the food of your [...]
blood; fill your servants whom you [...]
appointed to keep your flock, with the spi[...]
of your love, that they may freely spend and
be spent for the salvation of your people. We
ask this in your name.

FOR THE CHURCH

Eternal God, by your Son Jesus Christ you
established the family of your church in the
whole world: Breathe upon it anew the gifts
of your Holy Spirit, that in response to your
command it may go forth with strength to win
all people to the love of your name; through
our only Savior, Jesus Christ.

O God our Father, in whom is all quietness
and concord: Teach us to overcome all dissen-
sions within thy church which divide us from
one another and from thee; and by thy grace
make us all one in thee by the uniting power
of true faith and fervent charity, so that thy
church may patiently serve and glorify thee;
through Jesus Christ our Lord.

...ver and eternal... ...ir whole church,... ...mystery; by the... ...providence, carry... ...n of salvation; let... ...d know that things... ...are being raised up,... ...grown old are being made ne... ...ings are being brought to their perfection... him through whom all things were made, your Son Jesus Christ our Lord; who lives and reigns with you, in the unity of the Holy Spirit, one God, for ever and ever.

LORD, revive your Church, beginning with me.

FOR THE UNITY OF HUMANITY

Dear Father, bless peoples of all faiths and those of none, that we all may be given greater sensitivity to those who are different, deeper understanding of traditions other than our own, and a strengthened determination to work together for the sake of the whole human family.

FOR CHRISTIANS AND JEWS

O Lord our God, ruler of the universe, you have led your people ever since you called Abraham and made a covenant with him: Teach us to open our hearts and minds to our Jewish brothers and sisters; help us to learn more of our deep roots in their faith; and join us together in working and praying for the coming of your kingdom, through Jesus Christ our Lord.

FOR INTER-FAITH UNDERSTANDING

Grant, O God, that we may try to understand those of other faiths who are also seeking you. Help us, through word and deed, to witness to the self-sacrificing love of our Lord for every one of your children. We ask this for the sake of him who lived and died for all.

FOR CHURCH UNITY

O God of peace, through your Son Jesus Christ you set forth one faith for our salvation: Send your blessing upon all Christian people who are striving to draw nearer to you and to each other in the unity of the Spirit and in the bond of peace. Give us penitence for our divisions, wisdom to know your truth, courage to do your will, and love to break down barriers of pride and prejudice. Give us boldness to seek only your glory and the advancement of your kingdom.

Prosper the labors of all churches bearing the name of Christ and striving to further righteousness and faith in him. Help us to place the truth above our conception of it, and to recognize the presence of your Holy Spirit wherever you may choose to dwell; through Jesus Christ our Lord.

Grant, O Lord, that as there is one Spirit, one Lord, one faith, and one hope in our calling; so thy church being made again one Body, may draw all nations into unity; through him who wills that all should be one, even our Lord and Savior Jesus Christ.

SEND US

Send us, O God, as thy messengers, to hearts without a home, to lives without love, to those without a guide. Send us to the children whom none have blessed, to the famished who hunger, to the fallen whom none have lifted, to the bereaved whom none have comforted. Kindle thy flame in our hearts, that others may be warmed thereby; cause thy light to shine in our souls, that others may see the way; keep our sympathies and insight ready, our wills keen, our hands quick to help our sisters and brothers in their need; for Christ's sake.

FOR ORDAINED AND LAY MINISTRY

O God, you led your holy apostles to ordain ministers in every place: Grant that your church, under the guidance of the Holy Spirit, may choose men and women suitable for the Ordained ministry of Word and Sacrament, and, uphold them in their work for the extension of your kingdom; through him who is the Shepherd and Bishop of our souls, Jesus Christ our Lord.

God of faithfulness, in every age you call women and men to make known your love. May we be so strengthened in the ministries of love and reconciliation, to which we each are called by virtue of our baptism, that we may always witness to your holy name. This we pray in the name of Jesus Christ our Lord.

FOR A CHURCH CONVENTION

Almighty and everlasting Father, bless, we pray, with the presence of the Holy Spirit, those who make decisions for the renewal and mission of your Church. Grant them guidance to perceive what is right, courage to pursue it and grace to accomplish it; through Jesus Christ our Lord.

FOR STEWARDSHIP OF CREATION

O merciful Creator, your hand is open wide to satisfy the needs of every living creature: Make us always thankful for your loving providence; and grant that we, remembering the account that we must one day give, may be faithful stewards of your good gifts, through Jesus Christ our Lord.

FOR A
PARISH CHURCH

O God, make the door of this house wide enough to receive all who need thy Divine— and our—love and fellowship; and, narrow enough to shut out all envy, pride and strife. Make its threshold smooth enough to be no stumbling-block to children, nor to straying feet, but rugged and strong enough to turn back the tempter's power. God, make the door of this house the gateway to thine eternal kingdom.

Almighty and everlasting God, you govern all things in heaven and on earth: Grant to this parish and congregation all things we need; strengthen the faithful; arouse the indifferent; visit and relieve the sick; bless and protect the children; restore the penitent; and bring us all to be of one heart and mind, to the honor of your Name.

FOR OUR ENEMIES

O God, who hast taught us by thy Son to love our enemies and to pray for them: Grant them such knowledge of thee that no sin of ours may hide thy presence from them; and grant us so to love thee that we may forgive them and seek thy justice only, through the same Jesus Christ our Lord.

FOR MISSIONS

Almighty and everlasting God, the brightness of faithful souls, fill the world with your glory, we pray you; and show yourself, by the radiance of your light, to all the nations of the world; through Jesus Christ our Lord.

Lord Jesus Christ, you stretched out your arms of love on the hard wood of the cross that everyone might come within the reach of your saving embrace: So clothe us in your Spirit that we, reaching forth our hands in love, may bring those who do not know you to the knowledge and love of you; for the honor of your Name.

FOR THE CHURCH'S MISSION

Grant, O Father, that as we move among the people of your world, they may take knowledge of us that we have been with your Son, Jesus Christ.

Lord, open our hearts to receive your power; open our eyes to see Christ with hands outstretched to bless. Pour out your Spirit upon us and do with us what you will.

Draw your church together, O Lord, into one great company of disciples, together following our Lord Jesus Christ into every walk of life, together serving him in his mission to the world, and together witnessing to his love on every continent and island. We ask this in his name and for his sake.

O Lord, you have warned us that you will require much of those to whom much is given. Grant that we, who have received so much, may strive together, by our prayers, hard work and gifts, to extend to those who know you not what we so richly enjoy. So may your will be fulfilled with the salvation of all people.

O God, you have called men and women from every land to be a holy nation, a royal priesthood, the church of your dear Son: unite us in mutual love across the barriers of race and culture, and strengthen us in our common task of proclaiming the gospel of Christ to all the world, for the sake of the same Christ, our Lord and Savior.

O God, you have made of one blood all nations on the earth: We humbly thank you for revealing yourself in your Son, Jesus Christ; for those who have gone to the ends of the earth to proclaim the gospel to all people; and for those who heard and believed and now praise your name in every nation and language.

Almighty God, whose compassion fails not, and whose loving kindness reaches to the end of the world, we thank you for opening every land to the light of your truth and for planting your church in all the earth. Grant to your servants that we may labor abundantly to make known to all people your blessed gift of eternal life; through Jesus Christ our Lord.

FOR THE
FORWARD MOVEMENT

O God, we ask your blessing upon the Forward Movement of your church. Use it, we pray, to open our eyes to your glory and to the opportunities that lie before the church to reach people everywhere with the good news of Christ. Grant that the leaders of the Forward Movement may be both wise and daring disciples, and stir up in us the will to share joyfully in this work with our prayers and gifts. We ask this through Jesus Christ our Lord.

FOR MISSIONARIES

O God, our heavenly Father, we thank you for the gift of your dear Son. Grant that we who have received him in our hearts may joyfully go forth with him. Bless those who toil for you in far-off places. Comfort them in their loneliness, and unite our work to theirs. Accept our gifts, receive our prayers, and use us for the sake of your Son, Jesus Christ our Lord.

O God, you call men and women to carry the good news of Jesus Christ to all nations: Grant your strengthening grace to all who have responded to your call. Guide them in all their preparation, enriching the good gifts which they already possess and supplying those which they lack. Give them happiness and peace, insight and adaptability, courage and good judgment. Make them ready to learn as well as to give, that they may truly show forth your Son, not only in their words but in their lives.

FOR PEACE

Lord, let us have no other God before you; let us seek no other peace but the peace which is yours.

Eternal God, in whose perfect kingdom no sword is drawn but the sword of righteousness, no strength known but the strength of love: So mightily spread abroad your Spirit, that all peoples may be gathered under the banner of the Prince of Peace, as children of one Father; to whom be dominion and glory, now and for ever.

FOR PEACE AMONG NATIONS

Almighty God, kindle, we pray, in every heart the true love of peace, and guide with your wisdom those who take counsel for the nations of the earth, that in tranquillity your dominion may increase until the earth is filled with the knowledge of your love; through Jesus Christ our Lord, who lives and reigns with you, in the unity of the Holy Spirit, one God, now and for ever.

Almighty God, our heavenly Father, guide the nations of the world into the way of justice and truth, and establish among them that peace which is the fruit of righteousness, that they may become the kingdom of our Lord and Savior Jesus Christ.

FOR RESPONSIBLE CITIZENSHIP

O God, teach your people to rely on your strength and to accept their responsibilities to their fellow citizens. May they elect trustworthy leaders so that the rights of all may be protected and our nation be enabled to fulfill your purposes; through Jesus Christ our Lord.

FOR SOUND GOVERNMENT

O Lord our Governor, bless the leaders of our national, state and local governments, that we may be a people at peace among ourselves and a blessing to other nations of the earth. Grant to all in authority wisdom and grace in the exercise of their duties, foresight to provide for the needs of all our people, and courage to fulfill our obligations in the community of nations.

FOR OUR CROWDED CITIES

Heavenly Father, look with pity on our crowded cities; on the old, the ill, the lonely, the forgotten, hidden away in tenements, rooming houses and hospitals, and on children and young people exposed to all manner of evil. Stab our consciences awake to do all in our power to help with our prayers, our concern and our means to heal our society. We ask this through our Lord and Savior, Jesus Christ.

FOR SOCIAL JUSTICE

Almighty God, you created us in your image: Grant us grace fearlessly to contend against evil and to make no peace with oppression; and, that we may reverently use our freedom, help us to employ it in the maintenance of justice in our communities and among the nations, to the glory of your holy Name; through Jesus Christ our Lord, who lives and reigns with you and the Holy Spirit, one God now and for ever.

God of truth, protector of your people, come to the aid of all who are poor and oppressed. By the power of your life-giving word lead us in the ways of peace and integrity, and give us the help we long for in Jesus Christ our Savior.

FOR THOSE WHO LIVE ALONE

Almighty God, whose Son had nowhere to lay his head: Grant that those who live alone may not be lonely in their solitude, but that, following in his steps, they may find fulfillment in loving you and their neighbors; through Jesus Christ our Lord.

FOR REFUGEES

Lord Jesus, who as a child fled with your family to a strange country, look with pity upon the refugees scattered throughout the world. Save them from despair and give them hope. Grant that they may be welcomed to new countries and find new homes. We ask this in your Name.

FOR PERSECUTED
CHURCHES
AND CHRISTIANS

Give salvation and strength, O King of saints, to those who, being persecuted for righteousness' sake, are in great tribulation; and grant that these thy followers, loving not their lives unto the death and leaving all to follow thee, may overcome by the word of their testimony, and overcoming, may inherit all things.

FOR PERSECUTORS OF CHRISTIANS

Blessed Savior, who upon the cross didst pray for thy persecutors, saying "Father forgive them for they know not what they do:" Look upon them that in ignorance are now persecuting thy suffering sisters and brothers; open the eyes of them that are blinded by the powers of darkness, convince them of their sin, and bring them to repentance, that they may turn to thee and be saved.

FOR PRISONERS

Our heavenly Father, whose love and forgiveness are infinite, teach us that prisoners and captives are your children and our brothers and sisters. Help us to understand their misery and loneliness; may we go to them with compassion and words of hope, that they may not feel forsaken. Grant to all who work in prisons, in courts, and in other law enforcement agencies the wisdom to deal with mercy those who have gone astray; and may your Holy Spirit direct every effort to turn our penal system into one of redemption and hope. We ask it in the Name of him who came to save us all, Jesus Christ our Lord.

FOR THE RIGHT USE OF MONEY

Lord of our lives, teach us how to use our money and our possessions. Deliver us from stinginess or wasteful extravagance; inspire our giving with the spirit of true generosity. Help us always to remember your generous love for us, that we may be wise and faithful stewards of the good gifts you have given us; for your mercy's sake.

FOR VOCATION IN DAILY WORK

Almighty God our heavenly Father, you declare your glory and show forth your handiwork in the heavens and in the earth: Deliver us in our various occupations from the service of self alone, that we may do the work you give us to do in truth and beauty and for the common good; for the sake of him who came among us as one who serves, your Son Jesus Christ our Lord, who lives and reigns with you and the Holy Spirit, one God, for ever and ever.

FOR THE ADDICTED

O great Physician, who through your humanity entered into the sufferings of the sick, fill with your healing gifts all who are in any way addicted. Grant them your strength, your forgiveness, and your sustaining love. Of your mercy release them and restore them, that they may know the joy of life in your service.

O blessed Lord, you ministered to all who came to you: Look with compassion upon all who through addiction have lost their health and freedom. Restore to them the assurance of your unfailing mercy; remove from them the fears that beset them; strengthen them in the work of their recovery; and to those who care for them, give patient understanding and persevering love.

FOR SOCIAL SERVICE

Heavenly Father, whose blessed Son came not to be served but to serve: Bless all who, following in his steps, give themselves to the service of others; that with wisdom, patience, and courage, they may minister in his Name to the suffering, the friendless, and the needy; for the love of him who laid down his life for us, your Son our Savior Jesus Christ, who lives and reigns with you and the Holy Spirit, one God, for ever and ever.

FOR FAMILIES

Almighty God, our heavenly Father, who settest the solitary in families, we commend to thy continual care the homes in which thy people dwell. Put far from them, we beseech thee, every root of bitterness, the desire for personal glory, and the pride of life. Fill them with faith, virtue, knowledge, temperance, patience, godliness. Knit together in constant affection those who, in holy wedlock, have been made one flesh; turn the hearts of the parents to the children, and the hearts of the children to the parents; and so enkindle fervent charity among us all, that we be evermore kindly affected with holy love; through Jesus Christ our Lord.

FOR THE SICK

O Lord, holy Father, by whose loving-kindness our souls and bodies are renewed: Mercifully look upon these your sick servants. May every cause of sickness be removed, and may they be restored to soundness of health; through Jesus Christ our Lord.

Almighty God, look upon those who are sick in body or in mind: on the handicapped and the infirm; on all who suffer pain. Bless, O God, the ministrations of every one who gives them care; let your healing power be their invigoration, to restore them to health or alleviate their ills; let your loving-kindness be their solace; and grant them the faith, the patience and the valor by which the spirit serves the flesh and abides unconquered; through Jesus Christ our Lord.

FOR EDUCATION

Almighty God, the fountain of all wisdom: Enlighten by your Holy Spirit those who teach and those who learn, that, rejoicing in the knowledge of your truth, they may worship you and serve you from generation to generation; through Jesus Christ our Lord, who lives and reigns with you and the Holy Spirit, one God for ever and ever.

O Eternal God, bless all schools, colleges and universities, that they may be lively centers for sound learning, new discovery, and the pursuit of wisdom; and grant that those who teach and those who learn may find you to be the source of all truth; through Jesus Christ our Lord.

FOR ALL WHO SUFFER

O Lord, who dost feel the pain of the world, look down upon all sick and suffering persons; enfold them with thy love, that in the midst of pain they may find thy presence; to doctors and nurses grant tender hearts and healing hands; and give health again in body and soul, for thy tender mercy's sake.

FOR THE MENTALLY
AND EMOTIONALLY ILL

Most merciful and loving Father, with whom nothing is impossible, we pray that you will restore the light of reason and wholeness to those who are in mental or emotional darkness and despair. May your great love encompass them and may all discord and confusion be dispelled until your eternal peace and tranquility possess their souls; through Jesus Christ our Lord.

FOR THOSE WITH
INCURABLE DISEASES

O heavenly Father, we pray for those suffering from diseases for which at present there is no cure. Give them the victory of trust and hope, that they may never lose their faith in your loving purpose. Grant your wisdom to all who are working to discover the causes of disease, and the realization that through you all things are possible. We ask this in the Name of him who went about doing good and healing all manner of disease, your Son, Christ our Lord.

COMMENDATION AT
TIME OF DEATH

Depart, O Christian soul, out of this world;
In the name of God the Father Almighty
    who created you;
In the name of Jesus Christ who
    redeemed you;
In the name of the Holy Spirit who
    sanctifies you.
May your rest be this day in peace,
    and your dwelling place in the Paradise
    of God.

FOR THOSE IN SORROW

Almighty God, Father of mercies and giver
of comfort: Deal graciously, we pray, with all
who mourn; that, casting all their care on you,
they may know the consolation of your love;
through Jesus Christ our Lord.

FOR THE DEPARTED

O God, whose mercies cannot be numbered,
accept our prayers on behalf of the soul of thy
servant departed, and grant *him* an entrance
into the land of light and joy, in the fellowship
of thy saints; through Jesus Christ our Lord.

May the souls of the faithful departed, through the tender mercies of God, rest in peace. May light perpetual shine upon them. *Amen.*

THE COMMUNION OF SAINTS

Eternal Lord God, you hold all souls in life: Give to your whole church in paradise and on earth your light and your peace; and grant that we, following the good examples of those who have served you here and are now at rest, may at the last enter with them into your unending joy; through Jesus Christ our Lord.

FOR CHILDREN DEAR TO US

Lord, as once the mothers of Israel brought their children to you that you might bless them, so now we come to you, bringing with us in our hearts those children dear to us. We humbly entrust them to your never failing mercy and almighty love, asking only that they may do your will throughout their lives, and that you will keep them close to you for ever.

BENEDICTIONS

May the blessing of God Almighty, the Father, the Son and the Holy Spirit, rest upon us and upon all our work and worship done in his Name. May he give us light to guide us, courage to support us, and love to unite us, now and for evermore.

The God of peace, who brought again from the dead our Lord Jesus Christ, the great Shepherd of the sheep, through the blood of the everlasting covenant, make us perfect in every good work to do his will, working in us that which is well pleasing in his sight; through Jesus Christ, to whom be glory for ever and ever.

A CLOSING PRAYER

Almighty God, the fountain of all wisdom, you know our necessities before we ask and our ignorance in asking: Have compassion on our weakness, and mercifully give us those things which for our unworthiness we dare not, and for our blindness we cannot ask; through the worthiness of your Son Jesus Christ our Lord.

Times and Seasons

ADVENT

Almighty God, give us grace that we may cast away the works of darkness, and put on the armor of light, now in the time of this mortal life in which your Son Jesus Christ came to visit us in great humility; that in the last day, when he shall come again in his glorious majesty to judge both the living and the dead, we may rise to the life immortal; through him who lives and reigns with you and the Holy Spirit, one God, now and for ever.

CHRISTMAS

O God, you make us glad by the yearly festival of the birth of your only Son Jesus Christ: Grant that we, who joyfully receive him as our Redeemer, may with sure confidence behold him when he comes to be our Judge; who lives and reigns with you and the Holy Spirit, one God, now and for ever.

O God our Father, whose Word has come among us in the Holy Child of Bethlehem, may the light of faith illumine our hearts and shine in our words and deeds; through him

who is Christ our Lord, who lives and reigns
with you and the Holy Spirit, one God, now
and for ever.

Almighty God, who wonderfully created us
in your own image and yet more wonderfully
restored us through your Son Jesus Christ:
grant that, as he came to share in our humanity,
so may we share in the life of his divinity;
who is alive and reigns with you and the Holy
Spirit one God, now and for ever.

THE NEW YEAR

O Lord God of time and eternity, who makest
us creatures of time that, when time is over,
we may attain thy blessed eternity: With
time, thy gift, give us also wisdom to redeem
the time, lest our day of grace be lost; for our
Lord Jesus' sake.

EPIPHANY

Eternal God, who by a star led wise men to
the worship of your Son: Guide by your light
the nations of the earth, that the whole world
may know your glory; through Jesus Christ
our Lord, who lives and reigns with you and
the Holy Spirit, one God now and for ever.

THE ANNUNCIATION

Pour your grace into our hearts, O Lord, that we who have known the incarnation of your Son Jesus Christ, announced by an angel to the Virgin Mary, may by his cross and passion be brought to the glory of his resurrection; who lives and reigns with you, in the unity of the Holy Spirit, one God, now and for ever.

ASH WEDNESDAY

Almighty God, whose Son was revealed in majesty before he suffered death upon the cross, give us faith to perceive his glory, that being strengthened by his grace we may be changed into his likeness, from glory to glory; who lives and reigns with you and the Holy Spirit, one God, now and for ever.

Almighty and everlasting God, you despise nothing you have made and forgive the sins of all who are penitent: Create and make in us new and contrite hearts, that we, worthily lamenting our sins and acknowledging our wretchedness, may obtain of you, the God of all mercy, perfect remission and forgiveness; through Jesus Christ our Lord, who lives and reigns with you and the Holy Spirit, one God, for ever and ever.

HOLY WEEK

Lord Jesus Christ, Son of the Living God, we pray you to set your passion, cross, and death between your judgment and our souls, now and in the hour of our death. Give mercy and grace to the living; pardon and rest to the dead; to your holy church peace and concord; and to us sinners everlasting life and glory; for with the Father and the Holy Spirit you live and reign, one God, now and for ever.

Almighty God, whose most dear Son went not up to joy but first he suffered pain, and entered not into glory before he was crucified: Mercifully grant that we, walking in the way of the cross, may find it none other than the way of life and peace; through Jesus Christ your Son our Lord.

EASTER

Lord of life and power, through the mighty resurrection of your Son, you have overcome the old order of sin and death and have made all things new in him. May we, being dead to sin and alive to you in Jesus Christ, reign with him in glory, who with you and the Holy Spirit is alive, one God, now and for ever.

Creator of all, you wash away our sins in water, you give us new birth by the Spirit, and redeem us in the blood of Christ. As we celebrate the resurrection, renew your gift of life within us. We ask this in the name of Jesus Christ the risen Lord.

ROGATION DAYS

Creator of the fruitful earth, you made us stewards of all things. Give us grateful hearts for all your goodness, and steadfast wills to use your bounty well, that the whole human family, today and in generations to come, may with us give thanks for the riches of your creation. We ask this in the name of Jesus Christ the Lord.

ASCENSION

Almighty God, your Son Jesus Christ ascended to the throne of heaven that he might rule over all things as Lord: Keep the church in the unity of the Spirit and in the bond of his peace, and bring the whole of creation to worship at his feet, who is alive and reigns with you and the Holy Spirit, one God, now and for ever.

PENTECOST

Almighty God, who on the day of Pentecost sent your Holy Spirit to the disciples with the wind from heaven and in tongues of flame, filling them with joy and boldness to preach the gospel: Send us out in the power of the same Spirit to witness to your truth and to draw everyone to the fire of your love; through Jesus Christ our Lord.

TRINITY SUNDAY

Almighty and eternal God, you have revealed yourself as Father, Son and Holy Spirit, and live and reign in the perfect unity of love: Hold us firm in this faith, that we may know you in all your ways and evermore rejoice in your eternal glory, who are three Persons in one God, now and for ever.

THE TRANSFIGURATION

Almighty God, on the holy mount you revealed to chosen witnesses your well-beloved Son, wonderfully transfigured: Mercifully deliver us from the darkness of this world, and change us into his likeness from glory to glory; through Jesus Christ our Lord, who lives and reigns with you and the Holy Spirit, one God now and for ever.

ALL SAINTS' DAY

Almighty God, whose people are knit together in one holy church, the mystical Body of your Son: grant us grace to follow your blessed saints in lives of faith and commitment, and to know the inexpressible joys you have prepared for those who love you; through Jesus Christ our Lord, who lives and reigns with you and the Holy Spirit, one God now and for ever.

Preparation for
Holy Communion

To be said the night before Communion, or before the service on the morning of Communion.

PSALM 84

O how amiable are thy dwellings, thou LORD of hosts!

My soul hath a desire and longing to enter into the courts of the LORD; my heart and my flesh rejoice in the living God.

Yea, the sparrow hath found her an house, and the swallow a nest, where she may lay her young; even thy altars, O LORD of hosts, my King and my God.

Blessed are they that dwell in thy house; they will be always praising thee.

Blessed in the man whose strength is in thee; in whose heart are thy ways.

Who going through the vale of misery use it for a well; and the pools are filled with water.

They will go from strength to strength, and unto the God of gods appeareth every one of them in Sion.

O Lord God of hosts, hear my prayer; hearken, O God of Jacob.

Behold, O God our defender, and look upon the face of thine anointed.

For one day in thy courts is better than a thousand.

I had rather be a door-keeper in the house of my God, than to dwell in the tents of ungodliness.

For the Lord God is a light and defence; the Lord will give grace and worship; and no good thing shall he withhold from them that live a godly life.

O Lord God of hosts, blessed is the man that putteth his trust in thee.

Glory be to the Father, and to the Son, and to the Holy Ghost.

As it was in the beginning, is now and ever shall be, world without end. Amen.

Antiphon. I will fear no evil, for thou art with me; thou shalt prepare a table before me against them that trouble me: thou hast anointed my head with oil, and my cup shall be full.

Lord, have mercy upon us.
Christ, have mercy upon us.
Lord, have mercy upon us.

Our Father, who art in Heaven, Hallowed be thy Name. Thy kingdom come. Thy will be done, On earth as it is in heaven. Give us this day our daily bread. And forgive us our trespasses, As we forgive those who trespass against us. And lead us not into temptation, But deliver us from evil. *Amen.*

V. I said, Lord, be merciful unto me.
R. *Heal my soul, for I have sinned against thee.*

V. Turn thee again, O Lord, at the last.
R. *And be gracious unto thy servants.*

V. O Lord, let thy mercy lighten upon us.
R. *As our trust is in thee.*

V. Let thy priests be clothed with righteousness.
R. *And let thy saints sing with joyfulness.*

V. Cleanse thou me from my secret faults, O Lord.

R.   *Keep thy servant also from presumptuous sins.*

V.   O Lord, hear my prayer.
R.   *And let my cry come unto thee.*

V.   The Lord be with you.
R.   *And with thy spirit.*

Let us pray.

Most gracious God, incline thy merciful ears unto our prayers, and enlighten our hearts by the grace of thy Holy Spirit: that we may worthily serve at thy holy mysteries, and love thee with an everlasting love.

Almighty God, unto whom all hearts are open, all desires known, and from whom no secrets are hid; cleanse the thoughts of our hearts be the inspiration of thy Holy Spirit, that we may perfectly love thee, and worthily magnify thy holy Name.

Enkindle, O Lord, our hearts and minds with the fire of the Holy Spirit; that we may serve thee with a chaste body, and please thee with a clean heart.

We beseech thee, O Lord, that the Comforter, who proceedeth from thee, may enlighten our minds: and lead us into all truth, as thy Son hath promised.

Let the power of the Holy Spirit come upon us, O Lord, we beseech thee: that he may both mercifully cleanse our hearts, and defend us from all adversities.

O God, who didst teach the hearts of thy faithful people, by sending to them the light of thy Holy Spirit; grant us by the same Spirit to have a right judgment in all things, and evermore to rejoice in his holy comfort.

Purify our consciences, we beseech thee, O Lord, by thy visitation; that our Lord Jesus Christ thy Son, when he cometh, may find in us a mansion prepared for himself; who with thee, in the unity of the Holy Spirit, liveth and reigneth God, world without end.

Blessed Jesus, who art about to come to us thy unworthy servants in the Blessed Sacrament of thy Body and Blood, prepare our hearts, we beseech thee, for thyself. Grant us that repentance for our past sins, that faith in the atonement made for them by thee upon the Cross, that full purpose of amendment of life, that perfect love to thee and to all men, which shall fit us to receive thee. Lord, we are not worthy that thou shouldest come under our roof, much less that we should receive thee into ourselves; but since thou didst not disdain to be laid in a manger amidst unclean beasts, so vouchsafe to enter into our souls and bodies, unclean though they be through many sins and defilements. Lord, come to us that thou mayest strengthen us. And grant that having received thee, we may never be separated from thee by our sins, but may continue thine forever, till we see thee face to face in thy heavenly Kingdom, where, with the Father and the Holy Ghost, thou livest and reignest ever, one God, world without end.

Come, Lord Jesus, in the fulness of thy grace,
And dwell in the hearts of us thy servants;
That, adoring thee by faith,
We may with joy receive thee,
And with love and thankfulness abide in thee,
Our Guide, our Bread of pilgrims,
Our Companion by the way.

Thanksgiving After Holy Communion

Antiphon. Let us sing the song of the Three Children; which they sang as they blessed the Lord in the furnace of fire.

Benedicite, omnia Opera

All ye works of the Lord, bless ye the Lord: praise him, and magnify him for ever.

O ye angels of the Lord, bless ye the Lord: praise him, and magnify him for ever.

O ye children of men, bless ye the Lord: praise him, and magnify him for ever.

O let Israel bless the Lord: praise him, and magnify him for ever.

O ye priests of the Lord, bless ye the Lord: praise him, and magnify him for ever.

O ye servants of the Lord, bless ye the Lord: praise him, and magnify him for ever.

O ye spirits and souls of the righteous, bless ye the Lord: praise him, and magnify him for ever.

O ye holy and humble men of heart, bless ye the Lord: praise him, and magnify him for ever.

PSALM 150

Laudate Dominum

O praise God in his sanctuary: praise him in the firmament of his power.

Praise him in his noble acts: praise him according to his excellent greatness.

Praise him in the sound of the trumpet: praise him upon the lute and harp.

Praise him in the timbrels and dances: praise him upon the strings and pipe.

Praise him upon the well-tuned cymbals: praise him upon the loud cymbals.

Let every thing that hath breath: praise the Lord.

Nunc dimittis. St. Luke ii.29

Lord, now lettest thou thy servant depart in peace: according to thy word.

For mine eyes have seen thy salvation,

Which thou hast prepared before the face of all people;

To be a light to lighten the Gentiles: and to be the glory of thy people Israel.

Glory be to the Father, and to the Son, and to the Holy Ghost;

As it was in the beginning, is now, and ever shall be, world without end. Amen.

> Lord, have mercy upon us.
> *Christ, have mercy upon us.*
> Lord, have mercy upon us.

Our Father, who art in heaven, Hallowed be thy Name. Thy kingdom come. Thy will be done, On earth as it is in heaven. Give us this day our daily bread. And forgive us our trespasses, As we forgive those who trespass against us. And lead us not into temptation. But deliver us from evil. *Amen.*

V. All thy works praise thee, O Lord.
R. *And thy saints give thanks unto thee.*

V. Let the saints be joyful with glory.
R. *Let them rejoice in their beds.*

V. Not unto us, O Lord, not unto us.
R. *But unto thy Name give the praise.*

V. O Lord, hear our prayer.
R. *And let our cry come unto thee.*

Direct us, O Lord, in all our doings, with thy most gracious favour, and further us with thy continual help; that in all our works begun, continued, and ended in thee, we may glorify thy holy Name, and finally, by thy mercy, obtain everlasting life. Amen.

Anima Christi

Soul of Christ, sanctify me;
Body of Christ, save me;
Blood of Christ, refresh me;
Water from the side of Christ, wash me;
Passion of Christ, strengthen me;
O good Jesus, hear me;
Within thy wounds hide me;
Suffer me not to be separated from thee;
From the malicious enemy defend me;
In the hour of my death call me,
And bid me come to thee,
That with thy Saints I may praise thee
For ever and ever. Amen.

Holy Father, I thank thee
For the gift of thy dear Son.
Praised be thou, Lord Jesus,
Who hast refreshed me with the Bread
    of Life.

And granted me to drink of the brook in
   the way.
May I go in the strength of this meat
Unto the mount of God.
Blessed Spirit, give us grateful hearts,
That we may live in thankfulness and praise.
Thanks be to God for his unspeakable Gift.

THE BEATITUDES

Blessed are the poor in spirit, for theirs is
the kingdom of heaven. Blessed are those
who mourn, for they shall be comforted.
Blessed are the meek, for they shall inherit
the earth. Blessed are those who hunger and
thirst for righteousness, for they shall be
satisfied. Blessed are the merciful, for they
shall obtain mercy. Blessed are the pure in
heart, for they shall see God. Blessed are the
peacemakers, for they shall be called sons of
God. Blessed are those who are persecuted
for righteousness' sake, for theirs is the
kingdom of heaven.

— *Matthew 5:3-10*

Special Offices and Litanies

INVOCATIONS TO CHRIST

O Son of Mary: Consecrate our homes.

Son of David: Cleanse our politics.

Son of Man: Rule the affairs of Nations.

Son of God: Give us eternal life.

Jesus the carpenter: Hallow our daily work.

Jesus the Christ: Deliver a world which
   waits for thee.

Jesus the Savior: Save us from ourselves.

Jesus the life-giver: Renew thy Church.

Word of God: Perfect thy creation.

Lord exalted at the Father's side: Raise us
   to live with thee in God.

AN ACT OF PENITENCE

*(Each phrase to be said slowly and to be followed
by the response: "May God Forgive Us," after
which a pause.)*

For easy-going, "moral" lives with no love
   for God,
> *May God forgive us.*

For thinking ourselves to be righteous while
   despising others,
For not entering the Kingdom ourselves, nor
   suffering others that are entering to go in,
For calling Christ "Lord," but disobeying him,
For loading heavy burdens on others and not
   helping them,
For light neglect of our most solemn vows,
For not seeing with our eyes, nor hearing with
   our ears, not understanding with our hearts,
For cold hearts toward God and our neighbor,
For sulking, and taking revenge upon the
   Church,
For quickness to resent, and slowness to forgive,
For gossip and slander, backbiting and making
   trouble,
For pettiness and insisting on our own way,
For hoarding what God has loaned us for
   stewardship,
For saying "peace, peace," when there is no
   peace,
For siding with the world, and deserting Christ,
For quieting the voice of our conscience,
For rejoicing when others fall into sin,
For prefering indulgence above sacrifice,

> Lord have mercy.
> *Christ have mercy.*

AN ACT OF RENEWAL

(Where any group in home or church would make a new beginning to go forward in the Way.)

Lord, behold this thy family in Christ, and grant us to be one in thy Presence.

Lord, renew us by thy Spirit.

Pardon what is amiss in us, confirm what is good, and order what we shall be.

Lord, renew us by thy Spirit.

Withdraw us from ways and allegiances which would estrange us from thee.

Lord, renew us by thy Spirit.

Give us a desire to learn the Truth, and quicken our hearts with understanding.

Lord, renew us by thy Spirit.

Day by day guide us to seek thee in thy Word, and by the power of prayer.

Lord, renew us by thy Spirit.

Show us what thou wouldst have us to do, and give us grace to fulfill the same.

Lord, renew us by thy Spirit.

Make us so thankful that we shall offer all we have and are in thy Name.

Lord, renew us by thy Spirit.

Unite us in the Spirit with all others who seek thee in the Word and by prayer.

Lord, renew us by thy Spirit.

Grant us constancy and courage that we may be found faithful in thy sight.

Lord, renew us by thy Spirit.

May God the Father, the Son, and the Holy Spirit give light to guide us, courage to support us, and love to unite us, now and forevermore. Amen.

AN ACT OF HOMAGE TO OUR RISEN AND ASCENDED LORD

V. Glory to thee, O Christ our ascended and ever present Lord, through whom we have access to the Father.

R. *Glory to thee who lovest us and hast loosed us from our sins.*

V. Glory to thee who hast reconciled us all in one Body unto God through thy Cross, so that we are no more strangers and sojourners, but fellow citizens with the saints in the household of God.

R. *Glory to thee who hast led captivity captive, and hast given gifts for the perfecting of thy saints.*

V. Glory to thee who dost redeem unto God with thy blood men of every title and tongue and people and nation.

R. *Glory to thee who art in our midst when we are gathered together in thy Name.*

V. Glory to thee who hast gone before to prepare a place for us in thy Father's home.

R. *Glory to thee, the author and finisher of our faith, that God in all things may be glorified. Amen.*

(This Act of Homage is suitable for responsive use in families, groups, and congregations.)

A REAFFIRMATION OF FAITH

V. Our help is in the Name of the Lord;
R. *Who hath made heaven and earth.*

V. Blessed be the Name of the Lord;
R. *Henceforth, world without end.*

V. Lord, hear our prayer;
R. *And let our cry come unto thee.*

Let us pray:

Strengthen us, we beseech thee, O Lord, with the Holy Ghost, the Comforter, and daily increase in us thy manifold gifts of grace; the spirit of wisdom and understanding, the spirit of counsel and strength, the spirit of knowledge and true godliness; and fill us, O Lord, with the spirit of thy holy fear, now and for ever. Amen.

Then shall all ask God's blessing in the following prayer:

Defend, O Lord, thy children with thy heavenly grace; that we may continue forever; and daily increase in thy Holy Spirit more and more; until we come unto thy everlasting Kingdom. Amen.

A LITANY OF THANKSGIVING

Almighty God, our heavenly Father, from whom cometh every good and perfect gift, we call to remembrance thy loving kindness and thy tender mercies which have been ever of old, and with grateful hearts we lift up to thee the voice of our thanksgiving.

For the life thou hast given us, and the world which we live,

We praise thee, O God

For the work we are enabled to do, and the truth we are permitted to learn; for whatever of good there has been in our past lives, and for all the hopes and aspirations which lead us on toward better things,

We praise thee, O God

For all the comforts and gladness of life; for our homes and all our home-blessings; for our friends and all the pure pleasures of social life; for the love, sympathy, and good-will of men,

We praise thee, O God

For the gift of thy Son Jesus Christ, and all the helps and hopes which are ours as his disciples; for the presence and inspiration of thy Holy Spirit, and for all the ministers of thy truth and grace,

We praise thee, O God

For communion with thee, the Father of our spirits; for the light and peace which are gained through trust and obedience, and the disquietude which befalls us when we disobey thy laws, and follow our own desires and passions,

We praise thee, O God

For all the discipline of life; for the tasks and trials by which we are trained to patience, self-knowledge, and self-conquest, and brought into closer sympathy with our suffering brethren; for troubles which have lifted us nearer thee and drawn us into deeper fellowship with Jesus Christ,

We praise thee, O God

For the sacred and tender ties which bind us to the unseen world; for the faith which dispels the shadows of earth, and fills the saddest, and the last moments of life with the light of an immortal hope,

We praise thee, O God

O God of all grace and love, we have praised thee with our lips; grant that we may also praise thee in consecrated and faithful lives; through Jesus Christ our Lord. Amen.

LITANY FOR A CHRISTIAN HOME

O Father in heaven, we name our family after Christ, thy son. And for our dwelling, our food, our health, for all who serve our home—

We thank thee.

For making us dear one to another, for good times in happy union, and for all our many blessings—

We thank thee.

That thou wilt lead us day by day in ways of love and tenderness one to another—

We pray, Lord Jesus.

That each may stay close to all the rest; that we may be mindful one of another with sympathy and understanding—

We pray, Lord Jesus.

That honest and cheerful, brave and true, we may be quick and ready to help eath other meet the day's work and cares—

We pray, Lord Jesus.

That we may so respect and love each other that quarrels have no place in our tranquil home—

We pray, Lord Jesus.

For home life and its memories; for his keeping us one and secure; for him in whom we live and trust—

Bless we our God.

For his holy Church in all the world, God's greater family, that bid us share her gifts with God's children everywhere—

Bless we our God,
Father, Son, and Holy Spirit. Amen.

LITANY OF THE DISCIPLES' WAY

V. We are disciples of Christ and called by his Name. Let us draw unto him, who is the Living Way.

R. *Help us, O Master, to walk in thy Way.*

V. For our weakness and failures, grant us true repentance; and that we may TURN from self to thee.

R. *Help us, O Master, to walk in thy Way.*

V. Through each day's plans and choices grant us vision and courage to FOLLOW thee.

R. *Help us, O Master, to walk in thy Way.*

V. Grant us growing minds, that by eager study we may LEARN ever more of thee and of thy truth.

R. *Help us, O Master, to walk in thy Way.*

V. In joy and in sorrow, in victory or defeat, in all times and occasions, be thou our confidence and strength as we PRAY in thy Name.

R. *Help us, O Master, to walk in thy Way.*

V. Stir us to go forth and SERVE thee, thou who art one with all sufferers, the perplexed, and all who need.

R. *Help us, O Master, to walk in thy Way.*

V. In thy House and at thine Altar, in fellowship with thy people, grant us through WORSHIP new power to do thy will.

R. *Help us, O Master, to walk in thy Way.*

V. By thy gift on the Cross, by thine eternal self-giving, make us ready to SHARE with all who will receive.

R. *Help us, O Master, to walk in thy Way.*

A LITANY OF
PERSONAL CONSECRATION

In the Name of the Father, and of the Son, and of the Holy Ghost. Amen.

> Lord, have mercy.
> *Christ, have mercy.*
> Lord, have mercy.

Our Father...

That it may please thee to grant me by thy Holy Spirit to hear ever more clearly thy Voice, calling me to a deeper devotion to thy service:

O Lord, hear my prayer.

For grace to respond with my whole heart to thy call:

O Lord, hear my prayer

For a continual sense of thy abiding Presence and thy over-ruling guidance in my daily life:

O Lord, hear my prayer

For a deeper love and earnestness in the act of consecration to thee of myself, my soul and body, that I make anew at each Communion:

O Lord, hear my prayer

For the illuminating grace of thy Holy Spirit, that I may be guided to use for thee every power and every opportunity thou hast given me:

O Lord, hear my prayer

(The consecration of Love.)

For grace so to live in the light of thy Divine Love for me that, loving thee above all, I may give to others the sunshine of love which has its source in thee alone:

O Lord, hear my prayer

(The consecration of Friendship.)

For spiritual insight to realize more fully my influence on others, and grace to use it only and always for thee:

O Lord, hear my prayer

For wisdom taught of love to understand the needs of my friends, and grace to help them by prayer and sympathy:

O Lord, hear my prayer

(The consecration of Happiness.)

For a daily renewal of the spirit of true joy which the sense of thy abiding Presence alone can give, that all the joys of my life may be sanctified in Thee:

O Lord, hear my prayer

(The consecration of Trial.)

For a steadfast heart to meet with constant cheerfulness the anxieties and trials of my life, as thy way of sanctification for me:

O Lord, hear my prayer

(The consecration of Time.)

For inspiration and grace so to worship thee and to serve thee here, that I may be ready for thy perfect service hereafter:

O Lord, hear my prayer

For a right judgment in giving to each duty its due place and proportion, that my days may be ordered in accordance with thy Divine Will;

O Lord, hear my prayer

(The consecration of Social Life.)

For grace to make the spirit in which I fulfill all social duties one with the spirit of my inmost life and prayers:

O Lord, hear my prayer

For grace to refrain from the unkind word, and from the unkind silence:

O Lord, hear my prayer

(The consecration of Intellect.)

For guidance so to use the intellectual ability thou hast given that I may continually go forward toward the fulness of that perfection which thou hast purposed for me:

O Lord, hear my prayer

(The consecration of Substance.)

For a spirit of willing self-denial that I may give gladly and freely for the work of thy Church at home and abroad:

O Lord, hear my prayer

For inward light to see how far short I have come of thy Divine purpose for me:

O Lord, hear my prayer

For a truer penitence, a firmer faith, a deeper devotion, a more perfect love:

O Lord, hear my prayer

For a fuller apprehension of thine infinite Love for me—of the Power of prayer—of the Joy of spiritual things—of the Glory that shall be revealed:

O Lord, hear my prayer

And grant unto me, unworthy though I am, a clear vision of the beauty of Holiness, and a sure confidence that in thy light and by thy grace I may at last attain to it, through Jesus Christ my Lord. Amen.

A LITANY OF INTERCESSION

Almighty God, our heavenly Father, who lovest all and forgettest none, we bring to thee our supplication for all thy children. For all whom we love, and for whom we watch and care.

We beseech thee to hear us, O God.

For all who have blessed us with kindness, led us with patience, and restored us with their sympathy and help,

We beseech thee to hear us, O God.

For all who have wished or done us ill, that thou wouldst turn their hearts to penitence, and ours to blessings,

We beseech thee to hear us, O God.

For all prisoners and captives, and all who suffer from oppression, that thou wilt manifest thy mercy toward them, and make the heart of man merciful as thine own.

We beseech thee to hear us, O God.

For all who bear the cross of suffering, the sick in body or in mind,

We beseech thee to hear us, O God.

For all those who are troubled by the sin or suffering of those thy love,

We beseech thee to hear us, O God.

For all who are visited by worldly loss that in the dark and cloudy day they may find their peace in thee,

We beseech thee to hear us, O God.

For all who are absorbed in their own grief, that they may be raised to share the sorrows of their brethren, and know the secret and blessed fellowship of the Cross,

We beseech thee to hear us, O God.

For all who are suffering because of their faithfulness to conviction and duty, that renunciation may bring strength; and sacrifice, joy; and that they may have thy grace, who seest in secret, and come at last to their reward,

We beseech thee to hear us, O God.

For all perplexed by the deeper questions of life, and over-shadowed with doubt, that light may arise in their darkness,

We beseech thee to hear us, O God.

For all who are tried by passionate temptations, or mean suggestions, that thy mercy may be their salvation,

We beseech thee to hear us, O God.

For all who are lonely and sad in the midst of others' joys, that they may know thee as their friend and comforter,

We beseech thee to hear us, O God.

For the infirm and aged, and for all who are passing through the valley of death, that they may find their strength in thee, and light at evening time,

We beseech thee to hear us, O God.

For all forgotten by us, but dear to thee,

We beseech thee to hear us, O God.

O God our Father, have regard to our intercessions, answer them according to thy will, and make us the channels of thine infinite pity and helpfulness, worthy to pray as or Master hath taught us: Our Father...

LITANY FOR THE RECONCILIATION OF ALL

O God, the Father of Heaven, who hast made of one blood all men upon the face of the earth;

Have mercy upon us.

O God, the Son, Child of Mary, who for love of thy brethren wast lifted up upon the Cross of shame;

Have mercy upon us.

O God, the Holy Ghost, by whose Pentecostal gift each man did understand the language of the other;

Have mercy upon us.

O Holy Trinity, wherein Three are One;

Have mercy upon us.

From the sins that divide us; from all class bitterness and race hatred; from forgetfulness of thee and indifference to our fellow men;

Good Lord, deliver us.

From the corruption of the franchise and of civil government; from greed and from the arbitrary love of power,

Good Lord, deliver us.

From the fear of unemployment and the evils of overwork; from the curse of child labor and the ill-paid toil of women,

Good Lord, deliver us.

From the luxury that enervates; from the poverty that stultifies,

Good Lord, deliver us.

From the prejudice, self-deception, and hardness of heart; from apathy and impatience; from wrong and resentment and wrong suspicion,

Good Lord, deliver us.

From all rebellion against the kingship of Christ,

Good Lord, deliver us.

By the tears thou didst shed for thy city,

We beseech thee to hear us, good Lord.

That it may please thee to inspire thy Church with the vision of the New Jerusalem, coming down from Heaven to men;

We beseech thee to hear us, good Lord.

That it may please thee to unite the inhabitants of every city, state, and nation, in the bonds of peace and concord;

We beseech thee to hear us, good Lord.

That there may be no decay, no leading into captivity, and no complaining in our streets;

We beseech thee to hear us, good Lord.

By thy labor as a carpenter,

We beseech thee to hear us, good Lord.

That thy followers may be strong to achieve industrial justice, and to bid the oppressed go free;

We beseech thee to hear us, good Lord.

That the labor movement in America may be confirmed in disinterested honor, and that employers of labor may fashion their dealings according to the law of equity;

We beseech thee to hear us, good Lord.

By the mystery of thine Incarnation and the indwelling of the Holy Spirit,

We beseech thee to hear us, good Lord.

That thou wilt help us to give to all men health of body and of soul;

We beseech thee to hear us, good Lord.

That it may please thee to forgive our enemies, persecutors, and slanderers, and to turn their hearts;

We beseech thee to hear us, good Lord.

That in all time of our temptation, self-control and sacrifice may never fail;

We beseech thee to hear us, good Lord.

That thy kingdom may come on earth;

We beseech thee to hear us, good Lord.

O Christ, hear us.
O Christ, hear us.

Lord, have mercy upon us.
Christ, have mercy upon us.
Lord, have mercy upon us.

O Lamb of God, that takest away the sins of the world;

Have mercy upon us.

O Lamb of God, that takest away the sins of the world;

Grant us thy peace.

Our Father...

The Grace...

Canticles and Psalms

PSALM 23

The Lord is my shepherd;*
    I shall not want.
He maketh me to lie down in green
                    pastures;*
    he leadeth me beside the still waters.
He restoreth my soul;*
    he leadeth me in the paths of
    righteousness for his Name's sake.
Yea, though I walk through the valley of
             the shadow of death,
I will fear no evil;*
    for thou art with me;
    thy rod and thy staff they comfort me.
Thou preparest a table before me in the
             presence of mine enemies;*
    thou anointest my head with oil;
    my cup runneth over.
Surely goodness and mercy shall follow
             me all the days of my life;*
    and I will dwell in the house of the
    Lord for ever.

                              — King James Version

THE SONG OF MARY
Magnificat

My soul doth magnify the Lord,*
    and my spirit hath rejoiced in God my
    Savior.
For he hath regarded*
    the lowliness of his handmaiden.
For behold from henceforth*
    all generations shall call me blessed.
For he that is mighty hath magnified me,*
    and holy is his Name.
And his mercy is on them that fear him*
    throughout all generations.
He hath showed strength with his arm;*
    he hath scattered the proud in the
    imagination of their hearts.
He hath put down the mighty from their seat,*
    and hath exalted the humble and meek.
He hath filled the hungry with good things,*
    and the rich he hath sent empty away.
He remembering his mercy hath holpen his
        servant Israel,*
    as he promised to our forefathers,
    Abraham and his seed for ever.

— Luke 1:46-55

PSALM 23

The Lord is my shepherd;*
    I shall not be in want.
He makes me lie down in green pastures*
    and leads me beside still waters.
He revives my soul*
    and guides me along right pathways
    for his Name's sake.
Though I walk through the valley of the
             shadow of death,
I shall fear no evil;*
    for you are with me;
      your rod and your staff, they comfort me.
You spread a table before me in the
             presence of those who
             trouble me;*
    you have anointed my head with oil,
    and my cup is running over.
Surely your goodness and mercy shall
             follow me all the days of
             my life,*
    and I will dwell in the house of the
    Lord for ever.

— Book of Common Prayer

PSALM 121

I lift up my eyes to the hills;*
    from where is my help to come?
My help comes from the LORD,*
    the maker of heaven and earth.
He will not let your foot be moved*
    and he who watches over you will
    not fall asleep.
Behold, he who keeps watch over Israel*
    shall neither slumber nor sleep;
The LORD himself watches over you;*
    the LORD is your shade at your right hand,
So that the sun shall not strike you by day,*
    nor the moon by night.
The LORD shall preserve you from all evil;*
    it is he who shall keep you safe.
The LORD shall watch over your going out
                and your coming in,*
    from this time forth for evermore.

PSALM 62

For God alone my soul in silence waits;*
    from him comes my salvation.
He alone is my rock and my salvation,*
    my stronghold, so that I shall not be
    greatly shaken.   *— verses 1-2*

THE FIRST SONG OF ISAIAH

Surely, it is God who saves me; I will trust
    in him and not be afraid.
For the Lord is my stronghold and my sure
    defense, and he will be my Savior.
Therefore you shall draw water with
    rejoicing from the springs of salvation.
And on that day you shall say, Give thanks
    to the Lord and call upon his Name;
Make his deeds known among the peoples;
    see that they remember that his Name
    is exalted.
Sing the praises of the Lord, for he has
    done great things, and this is known in
    all the world.
Cry aloud, inhabitants of Zion, ring out
    your joy, for the great one in the midst
    of you is the Holy One of Israel.

— Isaiah 12:2-6

Notes

Most of the prayers in this revised edition come directly, or were adapted from, the Book of Common Prayer1979 and The Manual of the Society of the Companions of the Holy Cross.

Some of the prayers from The Book of Alternative Services, Anglican Church of Canada, are based on prayers in *The Roman Missal,* © 1973, International Committee on English in the Liturgy, Inc.

Prayers not from these sources or otherwise noted are from the original edition of *Prayers New and Old.*

Page 9:
"Oh God, whose desire is...," from David Mace, *Whom God Hath Joined.* Reprinted with permission of Epworth Press, Manchester, England.

Page 13:
"Lord Jesus bless me when I rise...," from *A Book of Childhood Prayers and Verses,* compiled by Carolyn Martin, ©1983, Hodder & Stoughton, 47 Bedford Square, London WC1B 3DP, p. 59. Reprinted by permission.

"I am the child of God...," *Ibid.,* p. 118.

"Lord Jesus, watch me...," *Ibid.,* p. 59.

Page 14:
"Praise be to God...,"*Ibid.,* p. 194.

"Teach me to pray dear Lord,...," *Ibid.,* p. 112.

Pages 25-26:
"Blessed are you...," The Book of Alternative Services (BAS), Anglican Church of Canada, p. 695.

"Come, Lord Jesus...," *Ibid.,* p. 694.

Page 34:
"Gracious God, we know...," *Ibid.,* p. 291.

Page 41:
"Almighty God, your Son...," *Ibid.,* p. 366.

Page 45:
"Father in heaven, you gave...," The Alternative Service Book, 1980 (ASB), Church of England, p. 335.

Page 56:
"Almighty God, you call your church...," BAS, p. 380.

Page 62:
"God of faithfulness, in every age..." Adapted from a "prayer over the gifts" in BAS, p. 396.

Page 65:
"Draw your church together...," *Ibid.,* p. 676.

Page 83:
"O God our Father, whose Word...," BAS, p. 274.

Page 84:
"Almighty God, who wonderfully created...," ASB, p. 450.

"Eternal God, who by a star...," BAS, p. 280.

Page 85:
"Almighty God, whose Son...," *Ibid.,* p. 288.

"Almighty and everlasting God, you despise nothing...," *Ibid.,* p. 281.

Page 86:
"Lord of life and power...," *Ibid.,* p. 335.

Page 87:
"Creator of all, you wash away...," *Ibid.,* p. 338.

"Creator of the fruitful earth...," *Ibid.,* p. 396.

"Almighty God, your Son Jesus Christ...," *Ibid.,* p. 343.

Page 89:
"Almighty God, on the holy mount..." *Ibid.,* p. 418.

"Almighty God, whose people...," *Ibid.,* p. 428.

Index